Velvet Noses

Spirited Lessons from the Horses We Love

ALDA ELLIS

HARVEST HOUSE PUBLISHERS

EUGENE, OREGON

When the Almighty put hoofs

on the wind and a bridle on the lightning,

He called it a horse.

VELVET NOSES
Copyright © 2007 by Alda Ellis
Published by Harvest House Publishers
Eugene, Oregon 97402

ISBN-13: 978-0-7369-2102-2

Design and production by Koechel Peterson & Associates, Inc.,
Minneapolis, Minnesota

Printed in China

10 11 12 13 14 15 / LP / 10 9 8 7 6 5 4

CONTENTS

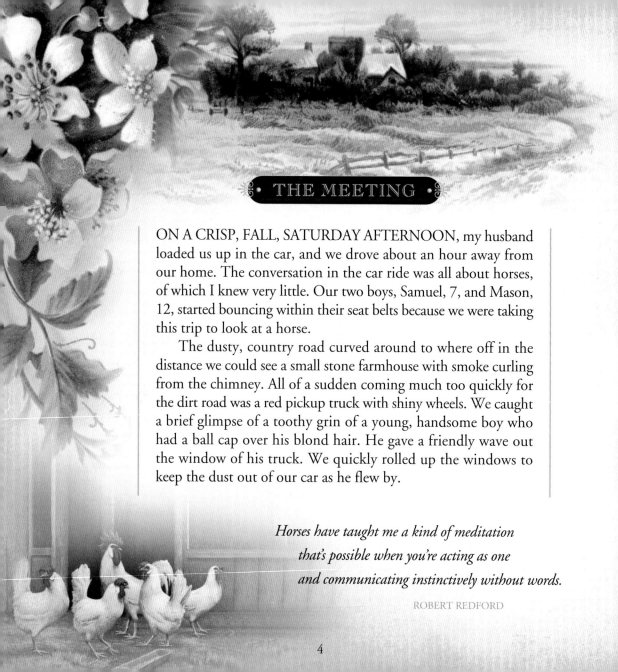

❦ · THE MEETING · ❦

ON A CRISP, FALL, SATURDAY AFTERNOON, my husband loaded us up in the car, and we drove about an hour away from our home. The conversation in the car ride was all about horses, of which I knew very little. Our two boys, Samuel, 7, and Mason, 12, started bouncing within their seat belts because we were taking this trip to look at a horse.

The dusty, country road curved around to where off in the distance we could see a small stone farmhouse with smoke curling from the chimney. All of a sudden coming much too quickly for the dirt road was a red pickup truck with shiny wheels. We caught a brief glimpse of a toothy grin of a young, handsome boy who had a ball cap over his blond hair. He gave a friendly wave out the window of his truck. We quickly rolled up the windows to keep the dust out of our car as he flew by.

Horses have taught me a kind of meditation
that's possible when you're acting as one
and communicating instinctively without words.

ROBERT REDFORD

When we pulled up in front of the farmhouse, Mr. Campbell met us outside with a hand extended toward my husband for a handshake. "I guess you met my son Will a minute ago," he said. "Can't slow that boy down; he just drives too fast. He was off to his softball game." Mr. Campbell glanced down at our two boys standing beside me, and he must have had a flashback because he said, "It was only yesterday my two boys were this age." He smiled.

"Well, I guess that is why you have a horse for us to look at then," my husband replied.

Mr. Campbell asked us to come on around to the back where a small, well-kept wooden barn was. A holding pen at the side of the barn held not one horse but three. The boys didn't wait for an invitation to the fenced-in area, and soon they were pulling handfuls of grass and offering them to the horses through the wooden fence. Three horses started toward us, and one by one tossed their velvet noses over the fence…and into our lives.

Each horse had a story, which the old farmer shared. The former "owners"—his sons—now preferred girls and baseball. Our sons were young and couldn't imagine a girl taking the place of a horse.

The world of horses was new to me, but I had listened for years to my husband's stories of the only other girl in his life whom he loved…his childhood horse, Dixie.

Mason and Samuel were soon jumping on their tiptoes with excitement as the two men firmed up their deal with a handshake. I was the quiet one, getting used to the idea of bringing a horse home. And now I, a city girl, was numb with the thought that we were bringing home three!

Three weeks passed, and the day before Thanksgiving a rusty, old horse trailer pulled into our pasture. Our new red barn was finished, the double crossbuck doors were open, and the barn was filled with hay. The old doors of the horse trailer opened wide with a clank, and we greeted, one by one, our new family members. Each horse walked down the planks differently, shedding light on the distinctive personalities.

Old Major was the first—the oldest and the slowest. We couldn't bear leaving this old horse all by himself after spending so many years with his best friends at his side. Separating these three horses was just not an option, so Old Major got a new home too. He happily spotted our tall, green grass and was immediately ready to eat.

Feisty Cheyenne was the smallest and youngest of the three. She was a full-blood American Paint, with dark brown and white colors. Her nostrils flared and the whites of her eyes showed. She was definitely not familiar with all this and extremely out of her comfort zone. Holding on to the lead rope, Mr. Campbell talked to her and tried to soothe her as he coached her down the ramp. Once she was safely off the ramp, he slipped the rope from around her neck, and she flew like lightning to get away from the trailer. She ran in a big circle and stood at the back of the pasture, looking back up to where Old Major was contentedly grazing away. Kicking her back legs up with a

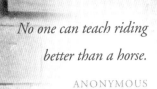

twist she turned and started running as fast as she could. She suddenly put on the brakes with dust flying, and simply stood near Old Major. Eating was most certainly not on her mind, for she glared at the trailer. Lifting her head, she let out a loud cry to her friend still waiting inside.

Mr. Campbell went back into the horse trailer to usher out the last horse. He slipped the lead rope around the great white horse's neck and patted him on the hip to turn. The last horse stood at the door of the trailer for a moment as if to announce, "Look at me. Here I am." The body language of this horse spoke volumes: the great one, the leader, the one who ruled. He too was an American Paint, mostly white with dark paintings on his hips and legs with white stockings. He was definitely the largest of the three. His ears pointed stiffly forward as he calmly looked over his new domain just as a general stands before his troops. Mr. Campbell didn't walk down the plank with the horse but simply slid the rope off the white horse's muscular neck.

"Here's Amigo," Mr. Campbell announced.

Even Old Major, with grass extending from both sides of his mouth, stopped eating for a moment to look up.

After assessing the situation, ever so slowly Amigo walked stately down the plank and headed over toward Samuel. My child who looked so tiny in the presence of this great white horse had in his pocket a fistful of oats from the barn. He held out his outstretched hand. Amigo gently ate the handful of oats off Samuel's flattened fingers.

My heart was beating fast because I knew the possible danger, and it beat even faster when Amigo walked over to me. I didn't have any oats. Horses monitor their surroundings through their senses of vision, smell, hearing, and touch. Amigo was just checking out his new family. He sniffed my sweater, and his soft, white nose nuzzled my neck—he was quite curious about my pearls. I have always known that my beloved dogs had cold noses, and it seems like one of my two boys often has a runny nose. But horses have velvet noses. I'd never known how wonderful the smooth, warm, velvety nose of a horse could feel against my cheek. It was then I fell in love with this great white horse.

I grew to love these three horses, and they grew to love me. Just like the other pets we adore, they came in a dazzling array of colors and patterns. God created each one amazingly different in looks and personality. Just like people, no two horses are alike.

I guide you in the way of wisdom
and lead you along straight paths.
When you walk, your steps will
not be hampered;
when you run, you will not stumble.

PROVERBS 4:11-12

EQUINE IDIOMS

Impatience: "Hold your horses."

Nonsense: "Horsefeathers."

Truth: "Straight from the horse's mouth."
(This is probably derived from the fact that a smart horse trader would look into a horse's mouth for himself to determine its age, rather than trusting the word of the seller.)

Not Thinking: "Looks like you've put the cart before the horse."

Pride: "Get off your high horse."

Hindsight: "It's always easy to remember that you should have closed the barn door after the horses have gotten out."

Not Being Direct: "You're takin' the long way around the barn."

A Mind of One's Own: "You can lead a horse to water, but you can't make him drink."

Old Age: "Long in the tooth."
(A horse's front teeth get longer with age.)

Ingratitude: "Never look a gift horse in the mouth."
(It would seem ungrateful to see how old the gift horse is by looking at its teeth.)

• THE LESSON OF FEAR •

FEAR CAN BE a good thing, and it is okay to be a little scared. The first few weeks that we were the new owners of three horses, a large blanket of fear surrounded me. As a city girl I was totally out of my element when it came to our new family members. The three horses looked so big, and our boys looked so small. I didn't want an orthopedic surgeon in my future, and I was constantly worried when the boys were around the horses.

A few riding lessons taught us all how to respect and care for our new charges. And slowly I realized that the more I was around these wonderful creatures, the more my fears melted away. I learned respect and communication was the key to safely enjoying these large, benevolent beings.

Fear became a wonderful teacher. Through daily inter-actions, I discovered that fear was normal when confronting something new. My world horizons were expanding. I learned to stay sharp and be keenly aware of each horse's personality. My dose of nervousness was a good thing because it kept me on my toes. I faced my fear, and I grew to respect and admire these magnificent animals.

There have been many occasions when fear has overtaken me. I was afraid to learn to swim. I was afraid to ride the school bus on the first day of school. Starting a business made me terrified. Being called on to make a speech caused panic. I was handed the diagnosis of breast cancer and sank to my knees. Losing both my parents gave me many sleepless nights. I walked through all these fearful things with God's help and the support of family and friends.

This verse from Joshua strengthened me: "Be strong and courageous. Do not be terrified; do not be discouraged, for the LORD your God will be with you wherever you go" (1:9). What comfort to know that we are never alone! There will be fear in our lives as we face new situations. Faith is knowing there will also be light where there is darkness.

When I am afraid, I will trust in you.

PSALM 56:3

11

THE DISCIPLE

ACROSS THE HIGHWAY from our farm is my neighbor's beautiful fenced pasture. Since Old Major died, we now have only two horses, Cheyenne and Amigo. My neighbor has two also. Most times you will notice that his horses are usually standing near each other, which might not look out of the ordinary. My neighbor Joe has placed a small silver bell on one of his horse's bridles, and I can hear the slightest tinkle from my front porch. I wondered why only one horse had a bell.

Leaning on the fence one day I asked Joe about the bell. He explained, "Take a look into the other horse's eyes, and you will see that ol' Dooley is almost blind with cataracts. But he can hear the bell on Jud, and that gives him a sense of security. My grandkids just love Dooley, and I just couldn't bear to put him down. From what I notice, he seems to be okay when he can hear the bell. Especially when it is time to go to the barn to eat. Both horses seem to find their way in just fine."

These horses are a fine example in the lesson of discipleship. When we need someone to show us the way, all we have to do is listen for God's voice. God places in our lives people to lead us and advise us when we need it most…if we listen. Other times perhaps we are to be the lead horses and guide others in their times of need. This is the principle of discipleship. I believe we are all appointed by God to be disciples. All of us can't be missionaries in jungles and deserts, but we can, in our own small way, become missionaries in our own backyard. Probably an old cowboy was the one to say, "You can lead a horse to water, but you can't make him drink." We are asked to show the way to God. No matter where we are in life, God never asks about our abilities, just our availability.

In faith we listen for guidance and then leave footprints to guide others, for no one should be left to walk the trail alone. May we all listen and tune our hearts to become disciples.

Whom shall I send, and who will go for us? Then said I, Here am I; send me.

ISAIAH 6:8 KJV

A man on a horse is spiritually,
as well as physically, bigger than a man on foot.

JOHN STEINBECK

❖ IT'S THE LITTLE THINGS ❖

WALKING DOWN THE HILL to our barn in the late afternoon is one of the nicer things I do during my day. I pause at the pasture gate and get immediately noticed by Amigo and Cheyenne. Sometimes if I am running a bit later than usual, they are standing patiently with their heads over the gate waiting for me. Cheyenne knows that I often bring a treat, and she wants to be first, but Amigo makes his dominant position known just by looking at her. She begrudgingly backs away and gives him a little spirited kick. Their big brown eyes look right into my heart as if to say, "Where have you been? Did I do something wrong?" And, of course, they haven't. They melt my heart with their devotion.

Your horse loves you;

　　not for your looks, but for your love!

He knows when you're happy,

He knows when you're comfortable,

He knows when you're confident,

And he ALWAYS knows when you have carrots.

AUTHOR UNKNOWN

I once saw a poster of a little Amish boy kissing his horse. The caption said, "Learn to enjoy the little things—there are just so many of them." My daily visit with the horses is one of my favorite "little things." As I unlatch the gate, Amigo gets ever so close to me and smells my jacket. A horse has a keen since of smell. Over the years I have bonded with this great white horse, and even though he looks so majestic, he is as sweet as a kitten. He knows I will scratch the special spot on his neck that feels so good. Cheyenne stands back, impatiently waiting, for she knows there's a carrot just for her. These little things mean a lot to them too.

I pushed the gate closed behind me and refastened the latch. As I slid in the pasture and looked over my shoulder, I expected Amigo to follow me, but he didn't. He was preoccupied with something. He swished and flicked his tail wildly. Stomping his foot, his distress was obvious. Trying to understand what was going on, I suddenly noticed a horsefly buzzing overhead. Finally the horsefly lit on Amigo's back. Standing on my tiptoes, I could swat it. Needless to say I was extremely cautious, for this muscular white horse had a look of fear in his eyes. The horsefly that could leave a nasty bite was eliminated by my lucky hit and lay on the ground motionless. I scratched Amigo's back, and he relaxed into my chest, knowing this pest was eliminated.

Oftentimes it is a little tiny danger that seeps into our spiritual life and creates a bit of havoc. A little thread of gossip, a handful of resentment, a moment of envy…these are all little pests of sin that can bite, sting, and need to be swatted out of our day.

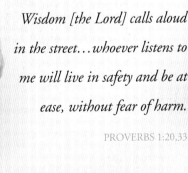

Wisdom [the Lord] calls aloud in the street…whoever listens to me will live in safety and be at ease, without fear of harm.

PROVERBS 1:20,33

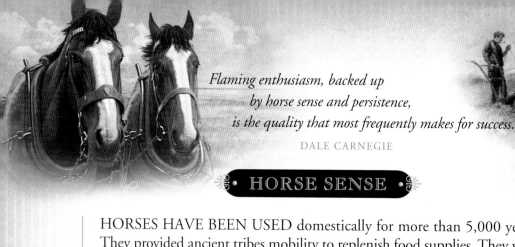

*Flaming enthusiasm, backed up
by horse sense and persistence,
is the quality that most frequently makes for success.*

DALE CARNEGIE

❧ HORSE SENSE ☙

HORSES HAVE BEEN USED domestically for more than 5,000 years. They provided ancient tribes mobility to replenish food supplies. They were used not only to hunt and ride, but were used to pull loads. The Egyptians used them to pull their chariots. The Persians used them to help build roads and domains. Horses played an important role in American history, being used by the Native Americans and the early pioneers as they helped to settle the American West. Poets, romantic writers, painters, photographers, and movie producers have immortalized them.

My father grew up not only riding horses, but also working behind them with a plow in the rocky fields to help make a living for a family of ten. Horses were lifelines to his family. They were the mode of transportation to get to school, to the store, and to church. Although each horse had a different personality, they all had "horse sense." Growing up, I often heard my father say, "He was an educated man, but he didn't have any horse sense." Now that I am grown with horses of my own, I know exactly what he meant.

GATHERING TOGETHER

One of the strongest traits a horse possesses is a herd instinct, whether there are 3 horses or 30. For horses in the wild there is safety in numbers when predators are about. And horses seem to prefer being with each other. There is an obvious internal comfort when they are with each other. They show their group instinct when you try to separate a horse from the others. Behavior in the herd is contagious, for when one gets excited and runs, they all get excited and run. When one starts to buck up, they all want to act up. Horses never lose this herd instinct. It can be controlled with patient training, but it is born in their souls. When training a young horse, it is good to let him mimic proper behavior as he moves along with a well-trained horse. Good behavior can be taught by example.

As Christians, we can apply the positives about being together in a herd to ourselves for attending and belonging to a church. Church is so important to us because we can support one another in time of crisis, offer fellowship with one another, and look to each other and our leaders for guidance. Our "herd" may be family, friends, and co-workers. As the mother of two sons, I knew the trouble they could get into by choosing the wrong circle of friends. But I also knew that the influence of great role models would guide them wisely. The herding instinct can be used to an advantage when training young horses and young Christians.

It's amazing to see how the horses we work with completely understand their job and take it seriously. We had one high-spirited pony named Bart that would practically get down on his knees to get close to the kids.

CLEA NEWMAN, *Pegasus Therapeutic Riding Program*

THERE'S NO PLACE LIKE HOME

Another trait of horses is their homing instinct. If you turn horses loose, they always go toward the stable or home pasture. The comfort of food and shelter is where they naturally want to return. Even Old Major knew when we were headed home after a long trail ride. His good sense of direction gave him a strong desire to head straight home. He instinctively knew the way home, and if I tried to go one more turn or circle around the field he tried to edge toward home...and the food he knew would be in his stall.

Wanting to be home isn't just a horse characteristic. In the years after my mother died, most evenings my husband would go after work to get my father, who lived nearby, so he could share in our family dinnertime meal. I loved having him at our dinner table because his stories were priceless. He gave our sons' listening ears a glimpse of life before cars, refrigerators, telephones, and iPods. In the summer we would sometimes spend the evening sprawled in Adirondack chairs down by the lake. We'd watch the horses and listen to a cicada serenade. Being with the horses seemed to bring our family closer together.

My father shared stories of riding a horse to school and of his father riding his horse as a young soldier in the Civil War. He spilled stories of grandparents driving their covered wagon down the Mississippi River Valley and the hardships involved. Stories of horse thieves and runaway buggies filled the nights. Sitting on cool evenings watching our horses brought a flood of memories and bits of family history that I would have never known if we had not gone to the lake to commune with Amigo, Old Major, and Cheyenne.

The following note was written by General Robert E. Lee to Markie Williams (Mrs. Lee's cousin) who wished to paint a portrait of Lee's famous and beloved horse, Traveller.

If I was an artist like you, I would draw a true picture of Traveller; representing his fine proportions, muscular figure, deep chest, short back, strong haunches, flat legs, small head, broad forehead, delicate ears, quick eye, small feet, and black mane and tail. Such a picture would inspire a poet, whose genius could then depict his worth, and describe his endurance of toil, hunger, thirst, heat and cold; and the dangers and suffering through which he has passed. He could dilate upon his sagacity and affection, and his invariable response to every wish of his rider. He might even imagine his thoughts through the long night-marches and days of the battle through which he has passed. But I am no artist, Markie, and can therefore only say he is a Confederate grey.

GENERAL ROBERT E. LEE

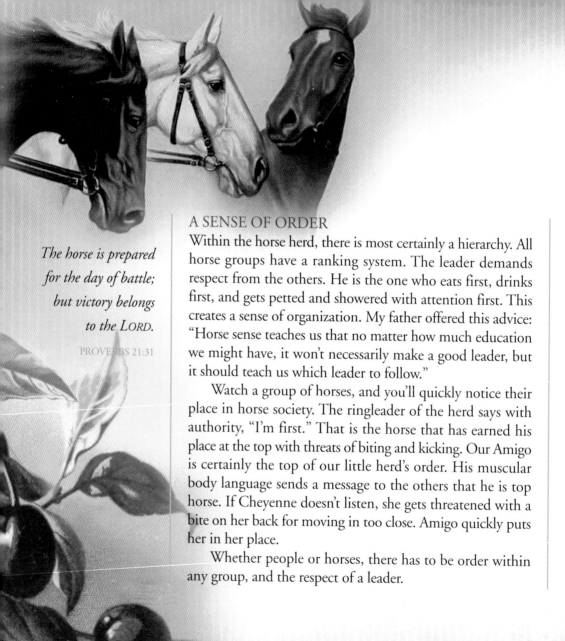

The horse is prepared
for the day of battle;
but victory belongs
to the LORD.

PROVERBS 21:31

A SENSE OF ORDER

Within the horse herd, there is most certainly a hierarchy. All horse groups have a ranking system. The leader demands respect from the others. He is the one who eats first, drinks first, and gets petted and showered with attention first. This creates a sense of organization. My father offered this advice: "Horse sense teaches us that no matter how much education we might have, it won't necessarily make a good leader, but it should teach us which leader to follow."

Watch a group of horses, and you'll quickly notice their place in horse society. The ringleader of the herd says with authority, "I'm first." That is the horse that has earned his place at the top with threats of biting and kicking. Our Amigo is certainly the top of our little herd's order. His muscular body language sends a message to the others that he is top horse. If Cheyenne doesn't listen, she gets threatened with a bite on her back for moving in too close. Amigo quickly puts her in her place.

Whether people or horses, there has to be order within any group, and the respect of a leader.

SECURE BUT FLEXIBLE

Horses are creatures of habit. It is one of their strongest traits, and just like us, they feel comfortable and secure when they do the same thing in the same way over and over. Good habits or bad habits, repetition naturally makes them feel more secure. Stepping out of routine takes them out of their comfort zone. Horses are so smart, and they have great memories. This means that they are very trainable. It's good to reinforce good habits, and change the routine to eliminate bad habits. This is true for horses and people.

It is always wise to pay attention to the horse's good sense. Sometimes when a horse won't do what you want—pay attention. The horse is probably being wise. For instance, a horse might refuse to walk in a slippery area. In the classic story *Black Beauty*, the horse refused to cross a bridge in the storm. Only later was it discovered that the bridge wasn't safe. Where do you go for your horse sense?

The horse has so docile a nature, that he would always rather do right than wrong, if he can only be taught to distinguish one from the other.

GEORGE MELVILLE

Horses change lives.
They give our young
people confidence
and self-esteem.
They provide peace
and tranquility to
troubled souls—
they give us hope!

TONI ROBINSON

One can get in a car
and see what man has made.
One must get on a horse
to see what God has made.

AUTHOR UNKNOWN

"No hour of life is lost that is spent in the saddle."

WINSTON CHURCHILL

• KEEP A CHILDLIKE QUALITY •

TODAY SOME HORSES are still used to pull carts and buggies, but for the most part in industrialized countries they are used for pure pleasure. The larger perspective of joy is the common ground shared by all those who love horses, no matter their preferred riding disciplines or events.

Recently our little friend Josie came again for a visit and brought a friend. These two sixth-grade girls decided they wanted to ride horses, and my husband was pleased to oblige because they had permission from their parents. Josie's friend was an accomplished rider and took the reins, soon getting Amigo into a nice trot and then a full gallop. Josie had never been on a horse before, and she held tight to the saddle horn as my husband led her around the pasture. Both girls giggled in delight with pure joy for love of these horses. They filled the air with laughter, and they had us all in smiles.

I was pleased that even though Josie had never been on a horse before, she was curious to try. That is a wonderful quality! Think of all the inventors that with a curiosity for experimenting and asking questions gave us great accomplishments from electricity to phones, from cars to computers. Whenever I spend a little time with Josie, she is right in my shadow and asking a million questions. Josie is very smart and she loves to read, but the only horses she has known have been on the pages of a book, so our farm is quite the adventure for her. Wonderful childlike curiosity is something that can't be taught in a book.

A HORSE'S EARS SIGNAL EMOTIONS

Ears pointed forward but relaxed	*The horse is interested in something in front of him.*
Droopy ears	*The horse is calm and relaxed. He may even be dozing.*
One or both ears forward, to the side, or slightly back	*The horse is relaxed yet paying attention.*
One or both ears moving quickly	*The horse is nervous about something.*
Both ears flat back against his neck	*The horse is angry. He might bite or kick. Get out of the way!*

AN ADVENTURE!

WHEN OUR OLDEST SON was little, we would go for a walk and he would ask, "Where are we going?" My answer was always the same: "We are going on an adventure!" Anytime my husband and I saddle up the horses, our boys know never to ask where we're going because they get the same answer: "I just want to go on an adventure." Today my business takes me out of town, and many times I am driving on unfamiliar streets and roads. When someone in the passenger seat asks, "Where are we going?" my answer is still the same: "We are going on an adventure!"

By going on an adventure, I mean that I will try to discover something new. On my adventure I am not looking for diamonds or gold. I am looking for wisdom and understanding. I am looking for and finding God in the world around me. Joy, curiosity, and adventure—they are gifts God's given us to make life worth living!

Boot, saddle, to horse,
and away!

ROBERT BROWNING

KINDNESS

Just like people, horses respond best to kindness. Horses, even though they are such big animals, are quite sensitive. They usually respond well to whispers and gentle touches. When properly trained, horses will do many different tasks at the slightest touch.

HOW TO GREET A HORSE

Always ask the owner if it is all right to pet the horse. Not only is it polite, the owner knows the temperament of his horse. Many horses are quite shy. Make friends by approaching slowly. Greet the horse with a gentle pat on the neck instead of his face. Their beautiful velvet noses are actually quite sensitive. The sense of smell is highly developed in the horse and serves primarily as a tool of recognition and to satisfy their curiosity. Let the horse smell you and proceed if his ears are forward and he's receptive.

Ninety percent of what goes
wrong is your fault.
You have to be smarter
than the horse.

NANCY CAHILL

You can tell a horse owner by the interior of their car.
Boots, mud, pony nuts, straw, items of tack, and a
screwed-up waxed jacket of incredible antiquity.
There is normally a top layer of children and dogs.

HELEN THOMPSON

*It's a lot like nuts
and bolts—
if the rider's nuts,
the horse bolts!*

MONTY ROBERTS